MACHINE
ACTION

A PRIMER FOR THE LAYMAN

ALAN T. NORMAN

TABLE OF CONTENTS

Table of Contents 2

Why I Wrote This Book 5
This book is not about coding machine learning algorithms .. 8
A primer for the layman 9

Chapter 1. What is machine learning? 11
Explicit programming vs. algorithm training 12
Definitions: Artificial intelligence vs. machine learning vs
neural networks 14
Basic concepts 17
    1. The Problem *17*
    2. The Data *19*
    3. The Algorithms *21*
    4. The Training *23*
    5. The Results *24*
Supervised vs unsupervised learning 25
    Supervised learning *26*
    Unsupervised learning *27*
    Semi-supervised learning *27*
What problems can machine learning solve? 28
The black box: what we don't know about machine learning
.... 29

Going Deeper 32

Chapter 2. Cleaning, labeling, & curating datasets .33
Cleaning the dataset 34
Need very large datasets for ML 34
    Learning curves *35*
    Cross-validation *36*
Need to be well-labelled 36
    Human-labelled data *38*

Synthetic data *39*

Chapter 3. Choosing or Writing a ML Algorithm 42

Basic concepts 43

Popular algorithm types 45

Linear Regression *46*

Logistic Regression *46*

Decision Trees *47*

Random Forest *47*

K-Means Clustering *48*

K-Nearest Neighbors *48*

Principal Components Analysis *49*

What it takes to write a novel algorithm 49

Chapter 4. Training & deploying an algorithm 51

Programming involved 51

Static vs dynamic 53

Tuning & feature engineering 54

Throwing an algorithm away 55

Chapter 5. Real-world applications of machine learning 57

Transportation 57

Product Recommendations 58

Finance 60

Voice Assistants, Smart Homes, & Cars 61

Conclusion 64

About The Author 65

Cryptocurrency Mining Bonus Book 66

Find the link to the Bonus Book below *66*

Other Books by Alan T. Norman: 67

WHY I WROTE THIS BOOK

Welcome to the world of machine learning!

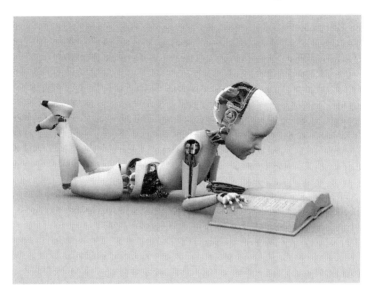

Artificial intelligence is poised to change the course of human history, perhaps more than any technology ever. A big part of that revolution is machine learning.

Machine learning is the science of teaching computers to make predictions based on data. At a basic level, machine learning involves giving a computer a set of data and asking it to make a prediction. Early on, the computer will get many predictions wrong. However, over the course of thousands of predictions, the computer will retool its algorithm to make better predictions.

This type of predictive computing used to be impossible. Computers simply couldn't store enough data or process it fast enough to learn effectively. Now, every year, computers are growing smarter at a rapid rate. Advances in data storage and processing power are driving this trend toward smarter machines. As a result, computers today are doing things that were unthinkable just a decade or two ago.

Machine learning is already affecting your daily life. Amazon uses machine learning to predict which products you'll want to buy. Gmail uses it to filter spam messages from your inbox. Your movie recommendations on Netflix are based on machine learning algorithms.

However, machine learning's impacts don't stop there. Machine learning algorithms are making predictions in all kinds of industries, from agriculture to healthcare. Moreover, its impacts will be felt in new industries and ways every year. As these new applications of machine learning emerge, we'll gradually accept them as part of normal life. Nevertheless, this new reliance on intelligent machines is a turning point in the history of technology, and the trend is only accelerating.

In the future, machine learning and artificial intelligence generally will drive the automation of a lot of tasks humans do today. Self-driving cars rely on machine learning for image recognition and they'll increasingly be a part of transportation, as will self-driving trucks and other vehicles to transport goods. Much of farming and manufacturing is now automated, so that machine learning is providing the food we consume and goods we use. The trend toward automation is only accelerating. Other machine learning applications could fundamentally change the jobs humans do day-to-day as machines become more adept at managing processes and completing knowledge work.

Since machine learning will have such a profound impact on everyday life, it's important that everyone has access to information about how it works. That's why I wrote this book. The current landscape for machine learning information is split.

First, there are explanations for the general public that dumb down the concepts. These explainers make machine learning seem like something only an expert could understand.

Second, there are the technical documents written by experts for experts. They exclude the general public with jargon and complexity. Obviously, writing and executing a machine learning algorithm is an enormous technical feat, and these technical explanations are important. However, there's a hole in the current literature around machine learning.

What about the layman who really wants to understand this technological revolution, not necessarily to write code but to have a grasp on the changes going on around him? Understanding the core concepts of machine learning shouldn't be confined to some technological elite. These changes will affect all of us. They have ethical consequences, and it's important that the public know about all the benefits and drawbacks of machine learning.

That's why I wrote this book. If that sounds interesting to you, I hope you enjoy.

THIS BOOK IS NOT ABOUT CODING MACHINE LEARNING ALGORITHMS

If that manifesto of an introduction wasn't clear enough: this isn't a book about coding. It's not meant for computer scientists to learn about how to create machine learning algorithms.

For one thing, I'm not nearly qualified to write a book like that. People spend years learning the intricacies of writing algorithms and training networks. There are entire PhD programs that explore the edges of the field, drawing on linear algebra and predictive statistics. If you dive deep into the details of machine learning and love it enough to get a PhD, you could easily come out making $300k-$600k working for a major tech company. That's how rare and valuable these skills are.

I don't have those qualifications, and I think that's a good thing. If you've picked up this book, it means you're a beginner interested in machine learning. You're probably not technical, or if you are, you're looking for a foundational book to get you started with the basic concepts. As a technology writer, I'm constantly learning about technologies. I'm a student of machine learning, and I remember what it's like to be a beginner. I can help explain the basic concepts in ways that are easy to understand. Once you've read this book, you'll have a solid grasp on the core principles that will make it easier to step to a more advanced book should you want to learn more.

That said, if you feel you already understand the core principles or you really want a book that can teach you the nuts and bolts of writing and training a machine learning algorithm, then this probably isn't the book for you.

A PRIMER FOR THE LAYMAN

The real goal of this book is to be an easy-to-read introduction to machine learning. My goal is to write a book that anyone could read, while remaining true to the principles of machine learning and not dumbing concepts down. I'm confident in the intelligence of my readers, and I don't think a beginner's book necessarily has to sacrifice complexity and nuance. That said, this isn't a big book, and it's nowhere near comprehensive. Those interested in the topic will want to go into greater depth with other books and research.

In this book, we'll look at the basic concepts and types of machine learning. We'll investigate how they work. Then, we'll explore the issues of datasets, and writing and training an algorithm. Finally, we'll see some real world use cases for machine learning and places where machine learning might be used next.

Once again, welcome to machine learning. Let's dive in...

CHAPTER 1. WHAT IS MACHINE LEARNING?

The goal of this first chapter is setting a framework for the rest of what you'll read in this book. Here, we'll nail down the basic concepts that we'll explore in greater detail in future chapters. This book builds on itself, and this chapter is the barebones.

That said, the logical place to start is by defining what we mean when we talk about machine learning.

MACHINE LEARNING

My simple definition goes like this: machine learning allows a computer learn from experience.

That may sound trivial, but if you break that definition down, it has profound implications. Before machine learning, computers couldn't improve from experience. Instead, whatever the code said is what the computer did.

Machine learning, in its simplest explanation, involves allowing a computer to vary its responses and introducing a feedback loop for good and bad responses. This means that machine learning algorithms are fundamentally different from the computer programs that have come before them. Understanding the difference between explicit programming and algorithm training is the first step to seeing how machine learning fundamentally changes computer science.

EXPLICIT PROGRAMMING VS. ALGORITHM TRAINING

With a few recent exceptions, nearly every piece of software you've used in your life has been explicitly programmed. That means that some human wrote a set of rules for the computer to follow. Everything from your computer's operating system, to the internet, to apps on your phone has code that a human wrote. Without humans giving a computer a set of rules to act, the computer wouldn't be able to do anything.

Explicit programming is great. It's the backbone for everything we currently do with computers. It's ideal for when you need a computer to manage data, calculate a value, or keep track of relationships for you. Explicit programming is very powerful, but it has a bottleneck: the human.

This gets to be problematic when we want to do complex things with a computer, like asking it to recognize a photo of a cat. If we were to use explicit programming to teach a computer what to look for in a cat, we'd spend years writing code for every contingency. What if you can't see all four legs in the photo? What if the cat is a different color? Could the computer pick out a black cat on a black background or a white cat in the snow?

These are all things we take for granted as humans. Our brains recognize things quickly and easily in many contexts. Computers aren't so good at that, and it would take millions of lines of explicit code to tell a computer how to identify a cat. In fact, it may not be possible at all to explicitly program a computer to 100% accurately identify cats, because context can always change and mess up your code.

This is where algorithms come into play. With explicit programming we were trying to tell the computer what a cat is and make allowances for every contingency in our code. In contrast, machine learning algorithms allow the computer to discover what a cat is.

To start, the algorithm might contain a few key features. For instance, we might tell the computer to look for four legs and a tail. Then, we feed the algorithm many pictures. Some of the pictures are cats, but others may be dogs, trees, or random images. When the algorithm makes a guess, we'll reinforce correct guesses and give negative feedback for incorrect guesses.

Over time, the computer will use the algorithm to build its own model of what to look for to identify a cat. The components in the computer's model may be things we didn't even think of at first. With more reinforcement and thousands of images, the algorithm will gradually become better at identifying cats. It may never reach 100% accuracy, but it will be accurate enough to replace a human cat image labeller and be more efficient.

Algorithms are guidelines but they aren't explicit rules. They're a new way of telling a computer how to approach a task. They introduce feedback loops that self-correct over the course of hundreds or thousands of trials at a task.

DEFINITIONS: ARTIFICIAL INTELLIGENCE VS. MACHINE LEARNING VS NEURAL NETWORKS

This book is about machine learning, but that term fits within a larger context. Since machine learning is growing in popularity, it's getting a lot of news coverage. In those articles, journalists often use the terms artificial intelligence, machine learning, and neural networks interchangeably. However, there are slight variations between the three terms.

Artificial Intelligence

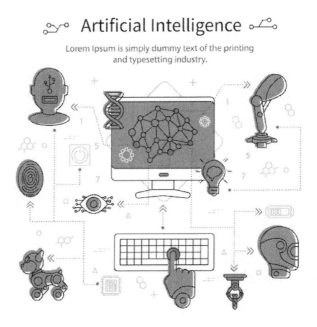

Lorem Ipsum is simply dummy text of the printing and typesetting industry.

Artificial intelligence is the oldest and broadest of the three terms. Coined in the middle of the 20th century, artificial intelligence refers to any time a machine observes and responds to its environment. Artificial intelligence stands in contrast to natural intelligence in humans and animals. Over time, however, the scope of artificial intelligence has changed. For instance, character recognition used to be a major challenge for

AI. Now, it's routine and no longer considered part of AI. As we discover new uses for AI, we integrate them into our frame of reference for what's normal, and the scope of AI extend to whatever the next new thing is.

Machine learning is a specific subset of AI. We've already spent some time defining it in this chapter, but it refers to giving a machine a feedback loop that allows it to learn from experience. As a term, machine learning has only been around since the 1980s. Only recently, in the past 10-15 years have we had the processing and data storage power to really start implementing machine learning at scale.

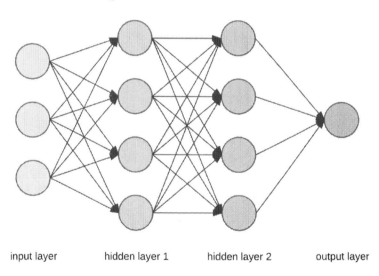

input layer   hidden layer 1   hidden layer 2   output layer

Neural networks are a subset of machine learning, and they're the hottest trend in the industry right now. A neural network consists of many nodes that work together to produce an answer. Each of the lowest nodes has a specific function. For example, when looking at an image the low-level nodes might identify specific colors or lines. Later nodes might group the lines into shapes, measure distances, or look for color density. Each of these nodes then gets weighted for its impact on the final answer. Early on, the neural network will make a lot of mistakes, but over the course of many trials it will update the weighting of each node to get better at finding the correct answer.

Now, when you read an article about AI, machine learning, or neural networks, you'll understand the difference. The key is to realize that they're subsets. Neural networks are just one type of machine learning which in turn is only part of artificial intelligence.

BASIC CONCEPTS

Machine learning can deploy in many uses cases. As long as there's significant data to analyze, machine learning can help make sense of it. As such, every machine learning project is different. However, there are five core parts of any machine learning application:

1. THE PROBLEM

Machine learning is useful anywhere you need to recognize patterns and predict behavior based on historical data. Recognizing patterns could mean anything from character recognition to predictive maintenance to recommending products to customers based on past purchases.

However, the computer doesn't inherently understand the data or the problem. Instead, a data scientist has to teach the computer what to look for using proper feedback. If the data scientist doesn't define the problem well, even the best algorithm trained on the biggest dataset won't yield the results you want.

It's clear that machine learning is not yet well suited to high-level, symbolic reasoning. For example, an algorithm may be able to identify a basket, colorful eggs, and a field, but it wouldn't be able to say that's an Easter Egg hunt, like most humans would.

Typically, machine learning projects have a very narrow, specific problem to which they're finding an answer. A different problem will require a new approach and possibly a different algorithm.

2. THE DATA

Machine learning is possible at scale because of the amount of data we've begun collecting over the past several years. This big data revolution is the key that has unlocked complex algorithm training. Data is at the core of tuning a machine learning algorithm to give the right response.

Since data is so central to machine learning, the results are a direct reflection of the inputs. If there's a bias within the data, the machine learning algorithm will learn to be biased. For example, applicant hiring predictors, court sentencing recommendations, and medical diagnosis are all using machine learning, and they all have some level of cultural, gender, race, education, or other bias built into the datasets that train them.

Bias extends beyond prejudice in data collection. Sometimes data misleads an algorithm in other ways. Consider the case of a military machine learning model trained to look for camouflaged tanks in a forest. The data scientists trained the algorithm on a set of pictures, some of which had tanks in the trees and others that just had trees alone. After training, the model scored nearly perfect accuracy on the tests the data scientists ran. However, when the model entered production, it didn't work at all to identify tanks. It turns out that in the training dataset, the pictures of tanks were taken on a sunny day, while the forest-only pictures were taken on a cloudy day. The algorithm had learned to identify sunny vs. cloudy days, not tanks!

No dataset is perfect, but we can take precautions to make them less biased. The key precautions come from statistics. When possible, data should be a random sample of the target population. The sample size should be large enough that you can draw meaningful conclusions from the results with a high level of confidence. Data should be accurately labelled and cleaned for bad/outlying data points that could mislead the algorithm.

We have an entire chapter to come on data, where we'll explore these issues in greater depth.

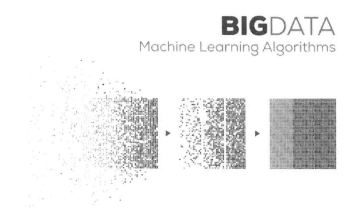

Algorithms are the major component that people think of when they reference machine learning. This is the actual code that tells the computer what to look for and how to adjust its weighting of possible answers based on the responses it receives.

There are many well-established machine learning algorithms at this point. Many of these come pre-loaded into popular data science coding libraries. Creating a basic machine learning model is as simple as testing multiple pre-created algorithms to see which fits the data best. Each model has its own strengths, weaknesses, architecture, and unique approach to weighting results.

If you're a programmer reading this book and thinking about getting into machine learning, don't make the mistake of writing algorithms from scratch. Eventually, yes, any good machine learning expert will need to know how to write an algorithm. However, the off-the-shelf algorithms are becoming industry standards and they work in 80+% of use cases.

Writing an algorithm from scratch requires significant math, theory, and coding skills. We'll have a whole chapter on algorithms and how they work, as well. Suffice it to say that the algorithms are the key to a working machine learning model.

4. THE TRAINING

Training an algorithm on a dataset is where the magic happens in machine learning. It's the part where the machine actually learns. It's also the part where machine learning can become resource intensive. If you're trying to do something complex or train an algorithm on a huge dataset, it could take time and significant computing power to get the results you want.

Training also generally comes with diminishing returns. For a given task with a yes/no answer, you can likely get to 80% accuracy with a small amount of training. To get to 90% would take much longer. 95% even longer, and each additional percentage of model accuracy you want the more training (and training data) you'll need. This algorithm tuning for accuracy is a major part of a data scientist's job.

Typically, machine learning training is static, meaning you can't train the model in real time. This means that the model is either in training or in production. With more use in production, the model doesn't get better. If you want to improve the model, you'll have to retrain it separately.

However, it is possible to dynamically train a model. These applications are much more difficult and expensive to implement. They also require that you constantly monitor the real-time data that the algorithm is receiving. The upside, of course, is the model remains responsive to incoming data and doesn't go out of date over time.

Another challenge is that during the training phase, the algorithm looks for correlation, not causation. A great example of this is the military tank camouflage detector I mentioned above. The algorithm found that cloudy days were correlated with getting the right result. Training teaches the algorithm to look for the right result, even at the expense of the right reasons. This is cool when machine learning points out a variable that correlates to correct results that we hadn't previously thought to look for. It's problematic when that correlation turns out to be a false positive of some kind.

We'll also have a full chapter on algorithm training later in this book. This chapter is just an outline of the basic concepts to get us started.

5. THE RESULTS

The final, often overlooked, step of machine learning is presenting the results. The goal of machine learning is to produce useful data for human beings. There's a lot of work a data scientist must do to explain the context, problem, and solution of a machine learning application. Aside from answering how and why the model works, the data scientists also needs to present results in a way that's accessible to the end audience.

In the case of Gmail's spam filter, that means demonstrating the spam-reducing value of the machine learning filter and building an integration for the model into the Gmail platform. For Amazon product recommendations, that means testing the results of the model in the real world.

Often, the act of preparing and using the results will uncover something that was missing in the original model. Thus, machine learning projects are often iterative, adding more functionality and combining various models over time to fit the needs of human beings in the real world.

SUPERVISED VS UNSUPERVISED LEARNING

Machine learning can be supervised, unsupervised, or semi-supervised. The various categories depend on the type of data and your goals for what to do with that data.

Supervised Machine Learning

The computer is given examples of inputs and typical outputs which it uses to develop and refine an algorithm. The algorithm is applied to new data and the outcome is used for further refinement. E.g. Training a computer to recognize and classify similar objects based on shape.

Unsupervised Machine Learning

Unsupervised machine learning is similar to learning without a teacher. The computer learns by exploring the data and finding structure and data patterns on its own. E.g. Learning to spot patterns in customer data based on purchasing behaviour.

SUPERVISED LEARNING

Supervised learning is the most commonly used and well-understood approach to machine learning. It involves an input and output for each piece of data in your dataset. For instance, an input might be an image and the output might be the answer to "is this a cat?"

With supervised learning, the algorithm needs a training dataset that's labelled with the correct answers in order to learn. Those labels act as a teacher supervising the learning. As the algorithm makes guesses about whether or not there is a cat in the picture, the teacher's feedback (the labels) will help the model tune itself. The model stops learning when it reaches an acceptable level of accuracy or runs out of labelled training data.

Supervised learning is great for tasks where the model needs to predict outcomes. These prediction problems could involve using statistics to guess a value (e.g. 20 kgs, $1,498, .08 cm) or categorizing data based on given classifications (e.g. "cat," "green," "happy").

UNSUPERVISED LEARNING

We use the term unsupervised learning when the training dataset doesn't have labels with a correct answer. Instead, we allow the algorithm to draw its own conclusions by comparing the data to itself. The goal is to find out something about the underlying structure or distribution of the dataset.

Unsupervised learning can be used for clustering problems, where the data ought to be organized into groups that are similar. We can also use it for association problems to find out which variables correlate with each other.

Semi-Supervised Learning

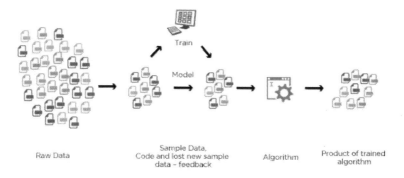

| Raw Data | Sample Data, Code and test new sample data - feedback | Algorithm | Product of trained algorithm |

In many cases, only part of the dataset is labelled, and that's where semi-structured learning comes in. When a majority of the dataset is unlabelled, usually due to the cost of hiring humans to label the data, we can still use a combination of supervised and unsupervised techniques to draw conclusions from the data.

Unsupervised learning can help us with the structure and distribution of the dataset. Then, we can use the few labels we do have as supervised training data. If we use that data on the rest of the dataset, we could potentially use the results as training data themselves for a new model.

27

WHAT PROBLEMS CAN MACHINE LEARNING SOLVE?

Let's take a look at some example problems that machine learning can address:

- Customers who bought x, are likely to buy y
- Fraud detection based on historical data
- Stock prediction and automated trading
- Identifying diseases in medical imagery
- Speech recognition for voice controls
- Predicting wine tasting ratings based on vineyard and climate data
- Predicting taste in music or tv shows (Spotify, Netflix)
- Combinatorial chemistry to create new pharmaceuticals
- Aircraft maintenance diagnostics
- Determining emotions and escalating incidents on customer support calls
- Self-driving cars (recognizing objects on the road)
- Facial recognition
- Micro-targeted marketing and advertising based on demographics
- Weather forecasting based on past patterns

Basically any application that involves classification, prediction, or detecting anomalies based on a large dataset is a potential use for machine learning. Machine learning is rapidly entering every aspect of our lives and over the coming years will be a foundational technology in society, in some ways like the Internet today.

THE BLACK BOX: WHAT WE DON'T KNOW ABOUT MACHINE LEARNING

If you read about machine learning, especially neural networks and deep learning, you'll likely hear references to machine learning being a "black box" model. When we talk about black boxes, we mean that the inner workings of the model aren't exactly clear. For example, the human brain is a black box decision maker (at least at this moment in history). We know certain parts of the brain are responsible for certain life functions. However, we don't really understand how the brain processes inputs and sends signals around to create thoughts and actions (outputs).

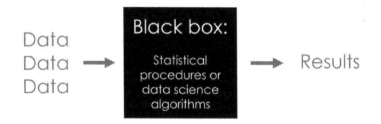

Similar complexity applies to some machine learning algorithms, especially ones that involve multiple layers of neural nodes or complex relationships between many variables. It can be difficult to explain, in a human way, what the algorithm is doing and why it works.

Of course, this black box terminology is somewhat of a misnomer in machine learning. We can, in fact, understand the architecture, patterns, and weights of the different nodes in an algorithm. Therefore we can look inside the black box. However, what we find there might not make any rational sense to us as humans.

Not even the foremost experts in the world can explain why a machine learning model has weighted and combined various factors the way it has, and in many ways it's highly dependent on the dataset the model was trained on. It's possible that an algorithm trained on a different training dataset could create a completely different model that still generates similar results.

To clarify, it's helpful to think of machine learning algorithms (in supervised learning scenarios) as searching for a function such that f(input) = output. When we use machine learning to model that function, the function is usually messy, complex, and we may not fully understand all the relevant properties of the function. Machine learning allows us to say exactly what the function is, but we may not be able to comprehend what the function does or why it does it.

In that sense, machine learning models can have black box problems where they're too complex to understand. But the entire field of machine learning is not necessarily a black box.

Still, the fact that we sometimes can't understand and explain the results of machine learning is troubling. As quickly as adoption of this technology is growing, machine learning is entering parts of our lives that have deep, lasting consequences. When a black box predicts treatment plans for diseases, runs an airplane's autopilot, or determines jail sentences, do we want to be sure we understand how those decisions are being made? Or do we trust the machines and the scientists behind the algorithms to look out for our best interests?

This is an ongoing debate at the heart of the machine learning revolution. On the one hand, trusting the algorithms and models could lead to saving lives, greater prosperity, and scientific achievements. However, the tradeoff in transparency is real. We won't be able to definitively say why our predictions are correct, only that the algorithm believes there's a 97.2% chance that they are.

I don't have an answer that can neatly tie up this debate. Instead, you'll have to form your own opinions based on the benefits and drawbacks you see in machine learning throughout this book and other reading. If you're interested in this problem, I recommend the MIT

Technology Review's "The Dark Secret at the Heart of AI" article (available online) to start learning more.

GOING DEEPER

Hopefully, this chapter has given a easy-to-digest, broad overview of how everything fits together and what to expect from each component chapter. In the following chapters we'll dig deeper into the nuts and bolts of machine learning.

Chapter 2. Cleaning, labeling, & curating datasets

After a data scientist defines a problem they'd like to solve, the first step in any machine learning adventure is finding a dataset that to work with. That may be harder than it sounds at first. While we're certainly living in the era of big data, finding clean data that's well-labelled for supervised learning with the necessary variables could be a challenge.

Choosing the right dataset, and having enough data for training, is critical to the success of a machine learning project. Data that's skewed or incomplete could lead to creating a machine learning model that's biased or outright useless.

The good news is there's a lot of potential data out there. Usually, when a data scientist works in a corporate setting, the company will already have some data that they want analyzed. This corporate data may also need to be linked to data from public sources.

For instance, satellite imagery from Landsat gets updated daily on Amazon Web Services, and you could track construction or deforestation with a machine learning algorithm. Open source mapping from OpenStreetMap could form the basis of a customer mapping problem. Information from the U.S. Census can give demographic information about an area. You can find human genomes sequenced and available to investigate genetic variation. Deutsche Bank releases real-time financial market data that would enable a machine learning project about market trends.

There's no shortage of potential projects. But before using all this data, data scientists have to be sure it meets a few criteria.

CLEANING THE DATASET

This is fairly straightforward, but failure to remove bad values will impact model performance. The first step to cleaning a dataset is removing any records that are missing key variables. Then, simple statistical methods help researchers identify and remove outliers. Other information that data scientists often remove include any time multiple columns are highly correlated. They also look for variables where the entire dataset shows near zero variance.

This data cleaning can often reduce a large dataset down to a fraction of its original size that's actually usable for machine learning.

NEED VERY LARGE DATASETS FOR ML

Some simple algorithms can learn on a small dataset. However, if you have a complex problem you want to solve with machine learning, you'll need a large training dataset. There are a few reasons why this is the case.

Small datasets can work successfully for machine learning when you use a model that has low complexity. However, the more nuanced you want your results to be, the more likely you are to overfit the model to the data. Overfitting is when the model makes broad assumptions based on limited data. It's called overfitting because the model will skew toward high, low, or otherwise outlying data points. The true answer might be somewhere closer to the middle, but since your dataset was limited, the model will bias captures the message and the noise training data. In essence, the model has learned the training data too well and has failed to get the general picture.

With more data, the model can get more accurate averages and begin to sort through the noise. That makes intuitive sense, but how do data scientists decide how much data is enough data?

Well, that answer is part statistics and part available computing resources. It also depends on the complexity of the algorithm.

LEARNING CURVES

When data scientists have too much data, they use something called a learning curve to plot the prediction accuracy vs. the size of the training set. For example, the algorithm may reach 80% accuracy after 100 training samples and 90% accuracy after 200 samples. Data scientists can keep going along that curve to see where accuracy maxes out, and how many training samples they'll need to get there.

Another consideration for whether you have enough data is cross-validation. In addition to the training data, data scientists set aside some of the original dataset for testing whether the algorithm is successful. For example, one common scheme is 10-fold cross-validation. The original dataset gets split into 10 equal groups. One group is set aside and the data scientists train the model using the remaining nine groups. Then, when model training is complete, they run the model on the data they set aside to test how accurately it performs.

Cross-validation takes more time because you have to train the models and then run them, often comparing multiple algorithms to see which performs the best. However, the extra time is worth it. Cross-validation is essential to building a successful machine learning model, since it allows researchers to identify and correct mistakes early in the process.

NEED TO BE WELL-LABELLED

For unsupervised learning, all you need is a good, large

dataset. From there, you can draw some conclusions about trends or clusters in the data. However, unsupervised learning applications are limited in the types of conclusions they can draw. For most machine learning applications where you'd like to use input variables to predict an outcome, then you'll need to perform supervised learning.

Supervised learning requires a dataset that's labelled with the correct answers. A simple way to think about it is the algorithm will make a guess, and then it will use the label to check its answer. If it gets the answer correct, the algorithm knows to increase the weight it gives to the factors that contributed to the right answer. If it gets the answer incorrect, the algorithm will decrease or otherwise adjust the weight it gives to the factors that produced the wrong answer.

Of course, the challenge is most data is not labelled. Companies and governments collect an enormous amount of data every year, but that data doesn't conveniently come along with the answers. (If it did, there wouldn't be much use for machine learning or predictive statistics!) Before we can train a supervised learning algorithm, we need to add labels to the raw data in order to make it useful.

For instance, an algorithm might be working in computer vision and we need it to correctly identify stop signs. We may have a bunch of images, but we need to go through and label whether or not there is a stop sign in each of the images.

Labelling data can be one of the most expensive and time-consuming parts of training a machine learning algorithm. It's also a risk that poor or inaccurate labelling can introduce bias into the training dataset and compromise the whole project.

If the data doesn't already have labels, there are generally two ways we can add those labels.

HUMAN-LABELLED DATA

Often, we use machine learning to teach computers to do tasks that we humans are intuitively good at. The stop sign example is a good one. When we see an octagonal, red shape with STOP, we know what we're looking at. Our brains are great at understanding context. Even if we can't see the whole sign, it has graffiti on it, or it's at a weird angle, we can still identify a stop sign when we see one. Machines can't intuitively do that.

As such, often the best way to label datasets is for humans to do it. Data scientists employ real people to look thorugh datasets and do the job that eventually the computer will learn to do. It could be identifying stop signs in photos, estimating distances, reading words, recognizing facial expressions, interpreting maps, or even making aesthetic or ethical judgments. There's an argument to be made that data labeling could be the new blue collar job of the AI era. The demand for labelers will be so large as every new ML application requires a training dataset.

Human labellers are great at these tasks. However, compared to computers, they're slow. Paying real people to label data is also expensive, prohibitively so for some use cases. As we've already covered above, humans are also biased. If a labeler or group of labelers has a bias, then that bias will likely appear in the final model.

An additional consideration is sometimes humans aren't so good at labelling. They might misjudge or jump to conclusions. As humans, we're overconfident in our own opinions, sometimes at the expense of objective truth. When we deploy machine learning in more nuanced use cases, these are all considerations we have to take into account.

All that said, humans are still the best data labellers we have. However, there are now attempts to get computers to take part in the labelling portion of machine learning as well.

SYNTHETIC DATA

Synthetic data is an emerging field in machine learning. The basic idea is to use a computer to generate labelled datasets from scratch.

Take our stop sign problem, for example. We could model a stop sign in a 3D CGI environment. Then, we could render images of that CGI stop sign in different backgrounds, angles, and lighting conditions. The resultant dataset would have a wide amount of variation that we could control. It would already be labelled based on whether the stop sign appeared in the rendered image.

This approach is exciting because it allows us to make complex datasets very quickly. They come pre-labelled and formatted to be fed into an algorithm. We also know that the labels are objectively correct. We can measure various variables in the synthetic dataset to high precision.

Of course, there are drawbacks as well. The biggest challenge is domain transfer. These image renderings and other types of synthetic data need to have fidelity to the real word. Ultimately, the goal is for the machine learning model to work in the real world. The fear is that, if we train it on computer-generated data, then the model may be good at recognizing rendered stop signs, but not real ones. Solving these fidelity and domain transfer problems are a major challenge for advocates of synthetic data.

Synthetic data may not necessarily be cheaper than human-labelled data, either. Creating a synthetic dataset requires a high level of expertise. Paying such experts would involve a significant investment up front. Such an approach likely only makes sense when you need thousands of data points, as a synthetic data generation event can scale much more easily than human-labelled data.

Finally, synthetic data can't help with labels that are inherently human-based, like aesthetics or ethics. Ultimately, we'll likely end up with a combination of synthetic and human labelled data for supervised learning.

Chapter 3. Choosing or Writing a ML Algorithm

This chapter could get very messy and confusing very quickly. That's because machine learning algorithms rely on complex statistics and mathematics to drive their results. To truly understand ML algorithms you'd want to study supervised/unsupervised learning, topological data analysis, optimization methods, dimensionality reduction strategies, computational differential geometry, and differential equations. Since this is a book for beginners, however, and I'm by no means an expert on ML algorithms, I'll avoid the math and do my best to explain them simply.

There are entire PhD programs on the subject of machine learning algorithms. You could spend years becoming an expert in this field, so there's no possible way I could explain it all in a book chapter anyway. That said, if the contents of this chapter interest you, pursuing a PhD in machine learning could pay off big time. Tech companies are scooping up PhDs and offering them salaries of $300k-$600k to write the algorithms for the newest and best machine learning applications.

I don't have a PhD in machine learning, and if you're reading this book you're likely a beginner to the concepts, anyway. So, let's take a look at the most basic functions of a machine learning algorithm, without getting into the math.

BASIC CONCEPTS

We've already covered the fundamentals of how machine learning works. Now, let's dig a little deeper into what exactly an algorithm does with the data. Each algorithm is different, but there are some commonalities between them:

- ☐ Inputs - All algorithms need some sort of input data. In data science applications that could be as little as a single variable. More likely, however, the model will be learning the relationship between tens, hundreds, or even thousands of variables at any time.

  For more complex applications, like computer vision, we need ways to turn visual information into variables that the computer can understand. There are different approaches depending on the context and problem you're trying to solve. Needless to say, even inputting data to an algorithm can be complicated, before the machine even does any learning.

  Choosing or creating an algorithm is highly dependent on the data you have to feed it and the context.

- Output vectors - At the end of any machine learning project, you want some type of output. However, it's not always clear exactly what data you'll need to satisfy your project. Choosing output vectors can be more complicated than it seems at first.

  Of course, for many projects the output will be obvious depending on your objectives. Nevertheless, as machine learning enters areas that are more nuanced and ambiguous, choosing and coordinating outputs can be a task in itself. You can't choose the right algorithm for your project if you don't have a clear idea of your expected outcome.

- Adjustment - Machine learning algorithms use feedback loops to fit a model to the data. This can happen in different ways. Sometimes an algorithm will try a random combination of factors until one begins to work, and that combination will receive a higher weight in future training tests. Other times, the algorithm has a method built in for finding and fitting a trend in the data that gradually tunes over time.

  This is where data scientists have to be careful.

▢ Sometimes an algorithm learns to fit its training data too well. That is to say, the model has become too specific to the data that it was trained on and no longer predicts general trends or classifications in the real world. In essence, the algorithm has learned its training data too well. This is called "overfitting" and it's an important concept to understand in machine learning. When data scientists train models, they have to make sure that their models walk a fine line between making specific predictions and being accurate generally.

Data scientists spend a lot of time thinking about and adjusting their algorithms to mitigate overfitting. However, they also test multiple algorithms at once side-by-side to see which ones perform best after training.

A key part of choosing or writing an algorithm is understanding how the algorithm adjusts over time in response to training data. These feedback loops are often where the complex mathematics come into play to help the algorithm decide which factors contributed to its success and should therefore be more heavily weighted. They also help the algorithm determine how much to increase or decrease the weight of a contributing factor.

POPULAR ALGORITHM TYPES

Okay, so we've covered a general overview of how an algorithm functions. Let's look at some of the most popular ones to get more specific details about how each one works.

LINEAR REGRESSION

This is a simple algorithm that relies on concepts taught in most Statistics 101 classes. Linear regression is the challenge of fitting a straight line to a set of points. This line tries to predict the overall trend for a dataset and you can use the line to make a probability prediction for new data points.

There are multiple approaches to linear regression, but each at its core is focused on finding the equation of a straight line that fits the training data. As you add more training data, the line adjusts to minimize the distance from all data points. As such, linear regression works best on very big datasets.

This is a fairly simple type of algorithm, but one of the key maxims of machine learning is don't use a complex algorithm where a simple one works just as well.

LOGISTIC REGRESSION

If linear regression was a straight line on a 2D plane, logistic regression is its older brother that uses curvy powerful than linear regression, but it's also more complex.

Logistic regression can handle more than one explanatory variable. It is a classification algorithm, and its outputs are binary (a scale from 0 to 1). As a result, it models the probability (e.g. ".887" or ".051") that the input is part of a given classification. If you apply it to several classifications, you'll get the probability of the data point belonging to each class. Mapping these probabilities gives you a non-linear multi-planar curve known as a "sigmoid." Logistic regression the simplest algorithm for non-linear applications.

DECISION TREES

If you've seen a flow chart, then you understand the basic idea behind a decision tree. The tree sets out a set of criteria, if the first criteria is a "yes" then the algorithm moves along the tree to the yes direction. If it's a "no," the algorithm moves in the other direction. Decision tree algorithms fine tune the criteria and possible answers until they give a good answer consistently.

In modern machine learning, it's rare to see a single decision tree. Instead, they often get incorporated with other trees simultaneously to build efficient decision making algorithms.

RANDOM FOREST

Random forest is one type of algorithm that combines multiple decision trees. It introduces the concept of a "weak learner" to the algorithm. Basically, a weak learner is a predictor that does poorly on its own, but when used in concert with other weak learners, the wisdom of crowds produces a good result.

Randomly implemented decision trees are the weak learners in a random forest. Each decision tree learns as part of the algorithm implementation. However, an overarching strong predictor is also learning how to combine the results from the various trees.

K-MEANS CLUSTERING

This is an unsupervised learning algorithm that tries to group the data into k number of clusters. Although it's unsupervised, the data scientist does need to provide direction at the start. They'll set images or data points that should be the center of each cluster. In other words, data points that are archetypal of what the cluster represents. Over the course of training, all the images or data points get associated with the cluster they're nearest to. Eventually, these data points converge with their appropriate clusters.

There are other faster or more optimized methods for unsupervised clustering. However, K-means remains popular because it's well established, documented, and generally effective.

K-Nearest Neighbors

K-Nearest Neighbors (KNN) is a classification algorithm. It shares some similarities with K-Means Clustering, but it is fundamentally different because it's a supervised learning algorithm while K-Means is unsupervised. Hence the slight difference in terminology from clustering to classification. KNN gets trained using labeled data so that it can label future data. K-Means can only attempt to group data points together.

KNN compares new data points to the existing data points from the labeled training data set. It then looks for the "closest neighbors" to that new data and associates those labels.

Principal Components Analysis

Principal Components Analysis (PCA) reduces a dataset down to its main trends. It's an unsupervised algorithm that you would use on a very large dataset to understand the data in simpler terms. It reduces the dimensions of your data. However, it also focuses on great variance between the dimensions (or principal components) so you don't lose the original dataset's behavior.

WHAT IT TAKES TO WRITE A NOVEL ALGORITHM

We've covered a few of the major algorithms and there are several more that make up the core of machine learning theory. Beyond these core algorithms, however, it's rare for someone to invent something truly new. Typically, new algorithms are improvements upon existing theories. Or, they customize an algorithm for use in a new scenario.

Part of the reason that new algorithms rarely get invented is because it's really hard. Creating an algorithm requires a strong grasp on complex mathematics. It also requires extensive proofs and testing. Additionally, the low hanging and obvious algorithms have already been invented.

But that's not all. Good algorithms are both effective and efficient, a tricky combination to nail down. Machine learning is a computational problem with thousands of data points as much as it's a mathematics problem. Debugging algorithms can also be very difficult since it's not straightforward where things have gone wrong.

Whenever possible, a machine learning project should apply existing tested and reviewed algorithms. Coding your own algorithms from scratch or cobbling together a hybrid approach is frowned upon because it can introduce errors, slow results, or be buggy.

Sometimes, developers and data scientists will need to tweak or implement an existing algorithm in a new context. Or maybe an existing algorithm isn't fast enough for a desired application. However, most machine learning applications can use existing algorithms and libraries effectively without having to code from scratch.

CHAPTER 4. TRAINING & DEPLOYING AN ALGORITHM

This is the step where the actual machine learning happens. After preparing the dataset, data scientists select several similar algorithms they think might work to accomplish the task at hand. Now, the challenge is to train those algorithms on the dataset and compare the results.

Often, it can be hard to tell which algorithm will work the best for a machine learning application before starting. For that reason, the best practice is to train multiple algorithms at first, select one or a few that perform the best, and then tune those algorithms until you get one model that works best for your needs.

When we say "best" that could mean multiple things. Of course, we want the model to make accurate predictions, so accuracy is an important component. However, if the model is resource or time intensive to get those results, then it may make more sense to choose a simpler algorithm. We'll get slightly less accurate results, but they'll come much more quickly.

PROGRAMMING INVOLVED

Machine learning sits at the intersection of statistics, calculus, and computer science. Since we're dealing with machines we're going to naturally need to write machine learning instructions in a programming language. With the growth in interest in ML, it's quickly becoming an enormous area of growth for new software developers. Skills in machine learning are highly valuable

So far, we haven't talked about the programming languages and approaches that developers use to code and create their machine learning applications. This section will be just a brief overview of the major players.

Python is by far the most popular language for creating machine learning applications. It's also the most preferred language in developer surveys about machine learning. A large part of Python's success is its simplicity compared to other programming languages. In addition, Google's open source library of machine learning algorithms, TensorFlow, is Python-based. The resources and the community are strong for machine learning applications built on Python.

Java and C/C++ follow Python by a wide margin in popularity. They're older languages, and they allow for lower level optimization of the environment where the algorithm will be running. Java and C/C++ get used in a lot of applications, not just machine learning. This means there are a lot of developers out there who understand these languages. There are some machine learning libraries for these languages, though nothing on the scale of TensorFlow.

R is another programming language that often enters the machine learning conversation. It's a specialized language that's designed for data science applications. While R certainly has its place in machine learning, it's rare for a project to choose R as its main or preferred language. Instead, it's more of a complementary language to the ones listed above.

Of course, it's possible to write machine learning code in many different languages. There are other languages that specialize in certain areas of statistics, data science, or modelling. Julia, Scala, Ruby, Octave, MATLAB and SAS are all options that occasionally arise in machine learning projects. However, these languages are the exceptions rather than the rule.

STATIC VS DYNAMIC

Once you've picked a programming language and installed a library to help you implement the algorithms you want to run, you're ready to start training your algorithms.

There are two types of machine learning training. The first is static training that receives training offline and is then finished learning until data scientists initiate a new training session. The second is a dynamic training where the model continues to learn in production, indefinitely.

Static models are much easier to build. They're also easier to test for accuracy and tend to run into fewer issues in deployment. If your data isn't changing over time, or is changing very slowly, a static model is the way to go since it's cheaper and easier to maintain.

Dynamic models are much more work-intensive to implement. They also require constant monitoring of the incoming data to make sure it doesn't inappropriately skew the model. Since dynamic models adapt to changing data, they're much better at predicting things like markets or weather, where patterns are constantly in flux.

TUNING & FEATURE ENGINEERING

A data scientist's job doesn't stop with picking a handful of algorithms and letting them run. In order to get optimal performance the person programming the algorithm has to set the input parameters that will go into the algorithm. Since machine learning problems are often complex, it can be difficult to decide which parameters are relevant and how many to include.

Trying different combinations of parameters and refining the best mix is known as algorithm tuning. There is no absolute right answer here. Instead, each tuning job is a matter of matching the algorithm to the context it's being deployed in.

Another related concept to tuning is feature engineering. Sometimes, like in the case of image recognition, feeding a computer a stream of data isn't enough for it to make sense of what it's seeing. While deep learning and neural networks have made progress on the front of computers learning from images, feature engineering is a handy way to tell a computer what to look for. You might engineer a feature that helps a computer identify a straight line or the edge of an object. Since you manually coded that feature, it's not technically machine learning, but now the machine knows what to look for.

Engineering features can dramatically increase performance.

THROWING AN ALGORITHM AWAY

If everything goes well, then the result is a model that has learned to accurately make predictions, clusters, or classifications in your data.

However, the dark side of machine learning is algorithms that don't work. There is a lot of time and money going toward machine learning applications right now. Unfortunately, many of these applications will end up as duds.

Perhaps the algorithms were poorly chosen or implemented. More likely, the project doesn't have enough or the right type of data to be successful. It's underreported how often machine learning projects fail.

The frustrating thing is it can be difficult to tell why your project is failing. You could have tons of data and test and tune many algorithms to no avail. This is especially true with complex problems or algorithms that implement multi-layered neural networks or random forests. It's difficult to say where things went wrong. Sometimes, data scientists invest a lot of time in a project, only to find they need to throw everything away and start over with more, new, or different data.

This may seem like a strange section to include in a book that's so optimistic about machine learning. However, I think it's important to highlight the fact that there's still a lot we don't know about creating and using machine learning projects. Projects fail all the time and fixing them is hard. That's an important reality of machine learning. It's critical that we acknowledge that just because a machine learning model produces an answer doesn't mean it's always right or incontrovertible.

We should respect and admire machine learning as a tool. But in the end, it's just that: a tool.

CHAPTER 5. REAL-WORLD APPLICATIONS OF MACHINE LEARNING

Now that you've got a basic understanding of how machine learning works, it's interesting to take a look at everyday examples of machine learning that you may not have even recognized.

TRANSPORTATION

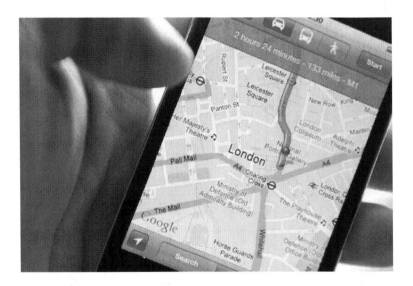

When you open Google Maps to get directions, you're using a dynamic machine-learning model. It uses anonymized cell phone data from drivers in your area to get commute times for various paths. The model also integrates data from Waze about road closures, accidents, and other user reports. Together, the model predicts the fastest route and estimated arrival time based on real-time information.

Lyft and Uber build on top of this data with their own machine learning algorithms that drive dynamic pricing and fare calculation. They also let you know how soon to expect a driver and when you're likely to arrive at your destination, even accounting for picking up and routing other people in the case of Uber Pool or Lyft Line ridesharing options.

These same routing, logistics, and arrival calculations also apply in long distance trucking, shipping, and even airplane navigation. Models help predict the fastest, safest way to transport goods and people while maximizing efficiency.

PRODUCT RECOMMENDATIONS

Basically any time a company makes a recommendation to you online, you can assume a machine learning algorithm helped make that prediction. Amazon knows what products you might be interested in based on what you've looked at and purchased before. Netflix knows what movies you'd enjoy because it learns from all the movies you've watched before.

Customers who bought this item also bought

Mastering Bitcoin for
Starters: Bitcoin and
Cryptocurrency...
› Alan T. Norman
⭐⭐⭐⭐☆ 166
Kindle Edition
$0.99

Blockchain Technology
Explained: The Ultimate
Beginner's Guide About...
› Alan T. Norman
⭐⭐⭐⭐☆ 76
#1 Best Seller in
Virtualization
Kindle Edition
$0.99

This goes deeper than just serving custom recommendations, it also applies to advertising. Facebook knows a ton of personal data about you, and they're using that data to customize which advertisements they show you. The same can be said for YouTube, Twitter, Instagram, and all other social media.

Additionally, Google uses your personal information to customize the results you receive when conducting a search. For instance, it is more likely to recommend local businesses in your town or articles from websites or writers that you've previously visited. Similar to social media, Google is also customizing its ads for you.

60

Don't believe me? Conduct a search on Google in your browser and then do the same search in an incognito window in your browser (gets rid of cookies and login information). For most searches, especially topics you've researched before, you'll see you're getting different results.

Even in-person machine learning will change the way we buy products. Major retailers are looking at computer vision applications that identify what you've already got in your basket and can make recommendations. Other systems are using facial recognition to identify when customers are lost or confused, and they can notify an employee to help. These systems are still in their infancy, but they represent the ways machine learning is integrating with every aspect of life, including human-to-human interactions.

FINANCE

Every major bank is using machine learning to help simplify their operations. In regulatory technology, machine learning algorithms can help banks identify if their processes and documentation are compliant to government standards. Other machine learning algorithms predict market trends or provide investment insights.

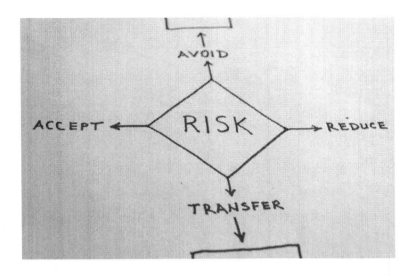

For loan applications or credit lines, machine learning can help banks predict the risk of lending to a given customer. These models can then suggest terms and rates that are individualized to the applicant. In banking, ML-powered character recognition makes it possible to deposit a check using your smartphone's camera. Machine learning can also detect and prevent fraudulent transactions from clearing on your account.

VOICE ASSISTANTS, SMART HOMES, & CARS

The likes of Siri and Alexa rely on machine learning to understand and respond to human speech. Conversational AI is the cutting edge of machine learning and neural network training. We've gotten pretty good at speech recognition and answering basic questions like "What will the weather be today?" The next challenge is getting a conversational AI that can talk about music, literature, current events, or other complex ideas.

The role of voice will only continue to expand over the coming years as we come to increasingly rely on our personal assistants. This is especially powerful when combined with the movement toward smart homes and autonomous vehicles. It's possible to imagine a future where you can control every aspect of your home and transportation intuitively by speaking with a voice assistant. In turn, each of these systems--like smart thermostats, intelligent security systems, and autonomous cars--use their own machine learning algorithms to perform the tasks we require of them.

CONCLUSION

Of course, there are tons of other use cases for machine learning in healthcare, manufacturing, agriculture, and everywhere else in our lives. Machine learning is useful anywhere there's data and we need help understanding, predicting, or using that data.

Machine learning is powerful, and it will continue to gain prominence in our daily lives. As such, it's important that everyone have a basic understanding of how it works, the potential flaws, and the enormous opportunities. Hopefully, this quick beginner's guide has provided a solid foundation for the layman interested in the basics.

That said, there's so much more to machine learning that isn't covered in this book! There are great resources available online and in print to expand your knowledge of this important technology even further. It's my hope that this is only the beginning of your machine learning journey.

Thanks for reading.

About The Author

Alan T. Norman is a proud, savvy, and ethical hacker from San Francisco City. After receiving a Bachelor's of Science at Stanford University. Alan now works for a mid-size Informational Technology Firm in the heart of SFC. He aspires to work for the United States government as a security hacker, but also loves teaching others about the future of technology. Alan firmly believes that the future will heavily rely computer "geeks" for both security and the successes of companies and future jobs alike. In his spare time, he loves to analyze and scrutinize everything about the game of basketball.

CRYPTOCURRENCY MINING BONUS BOOK

FIND THE LINK TO THE BONUS BOOK BELOW

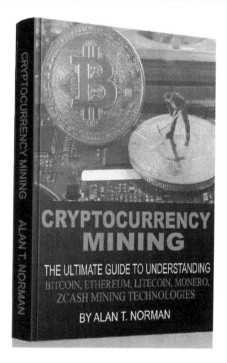

www.erdpublishing.com/cryptocurrency-mining-bonus/

OTHER BOOKS BY ALAN T. NORMAN:

Mastering Bitcoin for Starters
(http://amzn.to/2AwSNy0)

Cryptocurrency Investing Bible

(http://amzn.to/2zzB8IP)

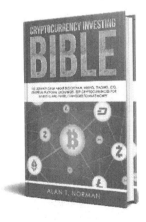

Blockchain   Technology   Explained

http://mybook.to/BlockchainExplained

Hacking: Computer Hacking Beginners Guide *(www.amazon.com/dp/B01N4FFHMW)*

Hacking: How to Make Your Own Keylogger in C++
Programming Language

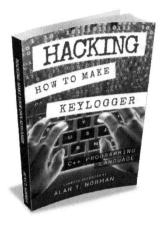

HACKED: Kali Linux and Wireless Hacking Ultimate
Guide *(https://www.amazon.com/dp/B0791WSRNZ)*

One Last Thing...

DID YOU ENJOY THE BOOK?

IF SO, THEN LET ME KNOW BY LEAVING A REVIEW ON AMAZON! Reviews are the lifeblood of independent authors. I would appreciate even a few words and rating if that's all you have time for

IF YOU DID NOT LIKE THIS BOOK, THEN PLEASE TELL ME! Email me at alannormanit@gmail.com and let me know what you didn't like! Perhaps I can change it. In today's world a book doesn't have to be stagnant, it can improve with time and feedback from readers like you. You can impact this book, and I welcome your feedback. Help make this book better for everyone!

Made in the USA
Middletown, DE
02 September 2018